# Whole Body Listening Larry at School!

2nd Edition

Elizabeth Sautter & Kristen Wilson

Illustrated by Eric Hutchison

Social Thinking

Think Social Publishing, Inc., Santa Clara, CA
www.socialthinking.com

**Whole Body Listening Larry at School! 2nd Edition**

Elizabeth Sautter and Kristen Wilson



Illustrations by Eric Hutchison, ehutch5@gmail.com

Edited by Ann L. Pendley, Ph.D., CCC-SLP

ISBN: 978-1-936943-32-6

Think Social Publishing, Inc.
404 Saratoga Avenue Suite 200
Santa Clara, CA 95050
Tel: (408) 557-8595
Fax: (408) 557-8594

This book was printed and bound in the United States by Mighty Color Printing.

TSP is a sole source provider of Social Thinking products in the U.S.

Books may be purchased online at www.socialthinking.com

**Thank you to:**
Susanne Poulette Truesdale for originating the concept of
whole body listening.

To Michelle Garcia Winner for her work and inspiration
in the area of Social Thinking.

And to the amazing therapists and clients with whom we work
at Communication Works in Oakland, CA; they inspire us everyday.

# What is Whole Body Listening?

Whole body listening is more than just "hearing" with the ears. It includes:

- listening with the eyes – looking toward the speaker
- listening with the ears – both ears ready to hear
- listening with the mouth – quiet and waiting for your turn to talk
- listening with the hands – quiet and kept to yourself
- listening with the feet – quiet and still
- listening with the body – facing toward speaker
- listening with the brain – thinking about what is being said
- listening with the heart – considering the speaker and others listening

Listening means much more than using our ears to hear what is being said. However, as adults we often forget to talk about what listening means and what it looks like. Children hear phrases from parents and teachers such as "pay attention" and "listen carefully" everyday. When adults make these requests children are not only expected to listen with their ears, but to stop whatever they are doing and demonstrate they are listening with their entire body. However, do we ever really say that or teach that to them? And, then what happens when the child doesn't show those behaviors? We feel frustrated and assume they aren't listening, don't want to comply, etc.

We need to understand that "listening" is an abstract concept, one that involves a complex set of skills for a child. Listening with your whole body involves integrating all of the body senses (sensory processing) and combining that with self control of our brain and body (executive functioning) and thinking of others and what they are saying and why (perspective taking). This is a complex task and it's extremely important to be aware of the levels of processing involved. Many children do not fully understand what is expected of them when we ask them to listen and some children may not be able to physically or cognitively meet the expected demands.

To make this abstract skill more concrete, in 1990 speech pathologist Susanne Poulette Truesdale created the concept "whole body listening" to explain how each body part is involved. Other professionals have expanded the initial whole body listening concept to include the heart as a way to encourage empathy and perspective taking. This later addition is helpful when working on social interactions and relationships in which the purpose of listening is not just to "hear" and interpret what is being said, but also to demonstrate shared involvement and to make a positive impression.

This expanded concept of whole body listening is woven into parts of Michelle Garcia Winner's larger Social Thinking® Methodology to teach the fundamentals of how and why we listen to figure out the "expected" behavior when around others. Similar to other Social Thinking Vocabulary that breaks down the social code, whole body listening has become a foundational concept to help make this and other abstract concepts more concrete and easier to understand, teach and practice.

Truesdale emphasizes that whole body listening is "a tool, not a rule," meaning that adults need to think flexibly about how best to use it. There is no "one way" to teach the whole body listening concept and there is no "one way" for children to demonstrate it. The goal is to create effective approaches for those with a variety of learning styles. And most importantly, to do this in ways that respect each person's particular needs and abilities. For instance, one child may have sensory issues that make it difficult for him to look and listen at the same time. Another child may not yet understand the use of body language and that people consider both her words and her actions when figuring out meaning in a social situation. She may be saying "I'm listening" but her body language may be sending a different message. Our kids with learning challenges, and even those without, may need adaptations or modifications made for them to feel and be successful demonstrating whole body listening. For more information on adapting the concept to different learners, please refer to the article, "Taking a Deeper Look at Whole Body Listening" (Sautter, 2015).

The book, *Whole Body Listening Larry at School*, was developed to help children understand the importance of attending and being part of a group. Paying attention and listening to others (adults, teachers, peers, etc.) are not only considered essential for social communication and social success, but are also fundamental abilities for learning to be part of a group and for academic success. In fact, these skills are clearly outlined in the Common Core and State Standards that teachers use to grade their students. They are also key components to schoolwide initiatives for PBIS (Positive Behavioral Interventions and Supports) that aim to create a positive and caring school culture among children, and for successful social emotional learning (SEL) skills. When an abstract concept such as listening is broken down and explained in a concrete, structured, and systematic manner, teachers are equipped with the tools to make this learning come alive for their students. The goal of this book (and its companion book, *Whole Body Listening Larry at Home*) is to do just that.

**How to Use this Book and Encourage Discussion**

The following are suggestions for teachers, therapists, and parents to consider while reading the book and to use at other times during the many natural teachable moments that arise throughout the day. These suggestions can be used with children with and without social challenges, including those with autism spectrum levels 1 and 2, ADHD, social communication disorders, social anxiety, twice-exceptional, hyperlexia, etc. or no diagnoses. We encourage you to modify any of these suggestions and create new strategies to use with your students that support their particular needs. Remember to consider each student's developmental and cognitive ability.

As you read the story:

- Take time to look at and talk about all the pictures in the book with your students. Make note of the characters' facial expressions, body positioning, thoughts and feelings. Discuss what it means to listen with each body part.

- As you move through the storybook, have students point out and then together discuss the body parts that are active and not active during whole body listening in each particular situation.

- To encourage self-awareness, and as it is appropriate within a group setting, discuss which parts of whole body listening are easier/more difficult for each student. For students who struggle with certain aspects of whole body listening, brainstorm tools and strategies for each body part.

- Talk about how the characters in the book feel when they are not listening or being listened to and why they feel this way. Ask your students to imagine how they would feel in similar situations. Be sure to explore listening from all angles: the child being listened to and not being listened to as well as the child listening/not listening to others. Some children may get frustrated when they are not being listened to, but don't realize when they themselves are not listening and are creating that same feeling in others.

- Widen their perspective to discuss the story from a teacher's point of view. For example, "This student looks bored" or "That student is distracted." Discuss how the teacher might feel as well as other classmates. Is it harder for the teacher to teach when students are not listening? How does one person's behavior affect other classmates and their ability to focus and learn?

- Before reading the story, discuss what it means to self-advocate when listening is or becomes difficult. Give your students phrases to use when they get to this point. For instance: "Can I take a short break?", "It's really hard for me to listen with my eyes in a small group" or "It's getting hard for me to keep my hands and feet quiet. Is it okay to listen from the back of the room so I don't disturb other students?"

Please refer to the end of the book for functional ways to teach and use the concept of whole body listening along with suggestions for accommodations to consider for individuals who struggle with this concept.

It's easier for me to teach when my entire class is listening with their whole body.

Hello class,
this is Leah and Luka—they are twins.
They are new students joining our school.
Please be friendly and
help them learn the rules!

Live
Magic!
Uh-oh, they don't know about whole body listening!
Buzzz-zz-zzz
Bzzzzz-zz

"Leah and Luka," Larry says, "now is not the time to be watching the flies.
You will miss the best part; try to listen with your eyes."

Children, please line up.

"Leah and Luka," Larry says, "Ms. Lang's voice is important to hear.
When recess has ended, remember to listen with your ears!"

And then the wizard picked up the magic wand...
The ants go marching one by one...

"Leah and Luka," Larry says,
"if we want to hear how the wizard sent the goblin south,
then please stop singing and listen with your mouth."

When we get to the music room, please choose an instrument to try.

"Leah," Larry says, "if you really want to be part of the band, keep your arms still and listen with your hands."

Listen carefully to this song we will learn to play.
STOMP!
STOMP!
STOMP!

"Luka," Larry says, "now is not the time to stomp to the beat.
Crisscross your legs and listen with your feet."

OK students, line up behind me so that we can find the next dinosaur.

“Leah,” Larry says, “now is not the time for practicing karate. You could get lost if you don’t listen with your body.”

The farmer wakes up early to feed all of the animals.

"Leah and Luka," Larry whispers,
"when we're in a circle, don't wonder about the rain.
Think about the story and listen with your brain."

My dog ran away yesterday.
We have a cat.

"Luka and Leah," Larry says,
"when you are talking with friends, caring is an important part.
Show them you are thinking about them and listen with your heart."

Listen with your eyes.
Listen with your ears.
Listen with your mouth...
...your hands.
Listen with your feet...
...your body.
Listen with your brain...
...and your heart!

"Wow!" Luka and Leah exclaim,
"Larry has taught us so much about how to listen with our eyes,
ears, mouth, hands, feet, body, heart, and brain.
We learned in our new school that whole body listening is super cool!"

I have no reason to complain when my students listen with their bodies and their brains.
I give them three cheers when they listen with their ears!

It's such a treat when they listen with their hands and feet.
My students are so wise when they listen with their mouths and eyes.
My friends are so thoughtful. It sets them apart when they listen with their hearts!

"Leah and Luka," Larry says, "look at their faces–that's how we know ...
... whole body listening is the way to go!"

# How to Teach and Implement Whole Body Listening at School

The following activities help adults introduce and reinforce teaching the whole body listening concept. As with other tools and curricula, the abilities and developmental level of each individual must be considered. Some of the skills used in whole body listening, such as maintaining eye contact, keeping one's body parts still, or remaining quiet, are extremely difficult and may cause stress or simply not be possible for certain people at certain times. When this is the case it's important that adults demonstrate awareness and understanding and make any needed modifications to help the student be successful in being part of the group.

**For early learners:**

- Make a copy of Larry and the body parts (eyes, ears, mouth, hands, feet, body, brain, and heart) from page 28 of the book. This same coloring page is available as a free download at either book's product page at www.socialthinking.com. Have students cut these out and then use them while discussing how each body part contributes to whole body listening. These can also be cut out from felt and used on a felt board.

- Use a potato head figure to demonstrate and discuss Whole body listening. Put the pieces of the body together. A hat can be used to represent the brain and a heart-shaped paper cutout to represent the heart. Have your students talk about how each part contributes to whole body listening.

- Play games that help build self-regulation such as red light, green light or freeze dance.

- Sing the song "Head, shoulders, knees and toes ...," but substitute the lyrics with body parts for Whole body listening (eyes, ears, mouth and hands, mouth and feet...).

- Play Simon Says and have students start by showing a wiggly, noisy body and then have them follow what "Simon Says" by listening with the various body parts. For instance, "Simon says, listen with your feet."

- Have students lie on their backs on a large piece of butcher paper. Trace an outline of their bodies and then have them label all the parts involved in Whole body listening. Post these visuals in class for their reference and review.

- Read books that show the characters using or not using Whole body listening. Two suggestions include *You are a Social Detective* by Michelle Garcia Winner and Pamela Crooke, and The *Berenstain Bears Go to School* by Stan and Jan Berenstain. Look for relevant illustrations and discuss what is going on in them. Next, ask your students to "teach" the characters about expected listening behavior using the whole body listening concept.

**For elementary grade students and up:**

- Provide visuals such as drawings or photos of various situations (e.g., an assembly, class story time, etc.) to give students a mental image and provide situational awareness for these contexts and expectations. The visuals in the book can be used for this as well. For more information on this idea, see the article "Using Whole Body Listening to Increase Executive Functioning" by Elizabeth Sautter and Sarah Ward (2013).

- Act out and role-play expected listening behavior in a given scenario, such as working in a small group. This provides more structure and a mental screenplay for students to practice within.

- Present a list of available group games. Once students have decided which one to play, have them practice using whole body listening during the game. Not all body parts are expected to be quiet or still while playing games (i.e., it's okay to move around during some games). Discuss students' thoughts and feelings about how this activity went for the group.

- If you have permission to take pictures or videos of your students for use in the educational setting, use video modeling to show them how well they're doing using whole body listening.

- Have students take on the role of teacher and discuss whole body listening in their own words with the class or other students. Give them different situations and have them figure out what is expected/unexpected listening behavior in each situation. They can also work in small groups to prepare a presentation with slides, video or poster that explains whole body listening to the class.

- Use a Social Behavior Map (Winner, 2007) to map out and discuss the expected and unexpected listening behaviors for various situations. Help students appreciate how each type of behavior affects others and ultimately the student when sharing space together.

- Make a small visual, a laminated card with all the body parts involved in whole body listening, to place on a desk or in a student's binder as a reminder.

## How to Encourage Whole Body Listening Across the Day

- Incorporate the whole body listening vocabulary into daily routines and make it a common language at school with students and other professionals.

- Send home information about whole body listening to students' families; encourage parents to use the vocabulary at home.

- Review expected listening behavior for students prior to each listening situation in the classroom. When more intense, focused listening is expected for an activity (e.g., reading or circle time), review all eight parts of whole body listening with the group. Remind them what each one looks like and why each one is important.

- Discuss how whole body listening applies to settings beyond the classroom, such as the playground, home, birthday parties, etc. Brainstorm different places where students can practice whole body listening.

- Before entering a social situation, prime, prepare and plan to set your students up for success. Discuss the hidden rules and expected behavior in the situation. For instance: during an assembly we listen with our hands and feet so we don't bump into the person sitting next to us. Once your students have a solid understanding of whole body listening, prior to entering a new or different situation, tell them that "sometime soon" or "in the next hour" they will have the opportunity to practice whole body listening. This primes their awareness ahead of time and gives students an opportunity to practice using the concept independently.

- Praise/acknowledge your students when they make their best effort to use whole body listening, are aware of their body, or use a tool and/or advocate for themselves. For instance: "I see you are listening with your hands," or "I like how you are trying to use your brain to think about what I am saying."

- Photocopy the Whole Body Listening Handout on page 28 and paste it on poster board for students to view. (As an alternative, purchase a larger poster from www.socialthinking.com.) You can also take a photo of the class (or a student) using whole body listening and paste that onto the poster. This can help students create their own mental image of what whole body listening looks like.

- Be mindful of individual students' strengths and challenges. If students have sensory and/or attention challenges be sure to provide breaks or movement to increase success during listening times.

- Teachers, parents, or other adults should be mindful and considerate of the readiness of a student to learn this concept. Do not "enforce" it on someone if it will cause anxiety, distress, or shame. When a child or adult is interested and capable of learning how to listen with his/her whole body it can be helpful to explore strategies and accommodations with the support team.

- Consider introducing mindfulness (being aware of the present moment), breathing exercises or other relaxation strategies to increase the mind-body connection and awareness.

References:


Berenstain, S. and Berenstain J. (1978). The Berenstain Bears Go to School. New York, NY: Random House.

Sautter, E. (2015). “Taking a Deeper Look at Whole Body Listening.” Social Thinking Publishing Newsletter, October 2015.

Sautter, E. and Kuypers, L. (2012). “Promoting Social Regulation.” Autism Bay Area, May-June 2012.

Sautter, E. and Ward, S. (2013). “Using Whole Body Listening to Increase Executive Functioning Skills.” Autism Bay Area, January-February 2013.

Truesdale, S.P. (2013). “Whole Body Listening Updated.”Advance for Speech-Language Pathologists & Audiologists, Volume 23, No. 3, 8-10. Available online at: http://speech-language-pathology-audiology.advanceweb.com/Features/Articles/Whole-Body-Listening-Updated.aspx

Truesdale, S. P. (1990). “Whole-Body Listening: Developing Active Auditory Skills”. *Language, Speech, and Hearing Services in Schools,* Volume 21, July 1990, 183–184.

Winner, M.G. (2007). Social Behavior Mapping. San Jose, CA: Think Social Publishing, Inc.

Winner, M. and Crooke, P. (2008). You are A Social Detective. San Jose, CA: Think Social Publishing, Inc.

# Handout for Whole Body Listening

Eyes – looking toward the speaker

Ears – ready to hear

Mouth – quiet and waiting for your turn to talk

Hands – quiet and kept to yourself

Feet – quiet and still

Body – facing toward the speaker

Brain – thinking about what is being said

Heart – considering the speaker and others listening

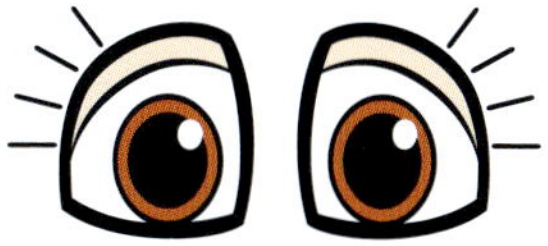

eyes watching

ears listening

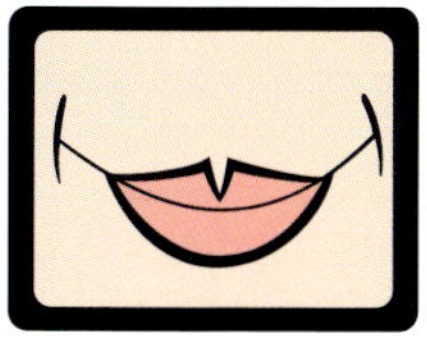

mouth quiet

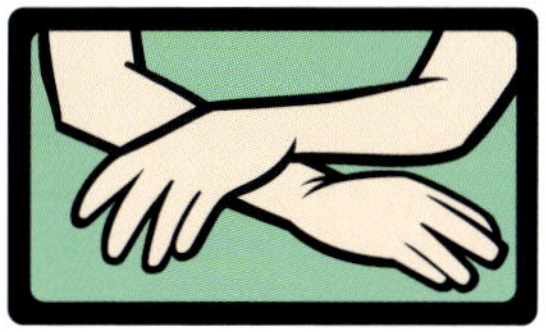

hands still

feet still

body facing speaker

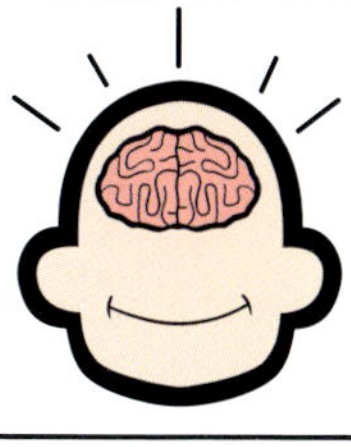

brain thinking

heart caring

**Download a free Whole Body Listening Larry coloring page at the book's product description page.**

**www.socialthinking.com**

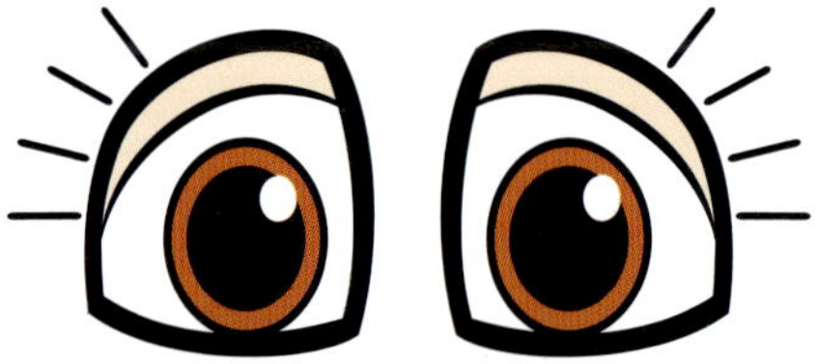

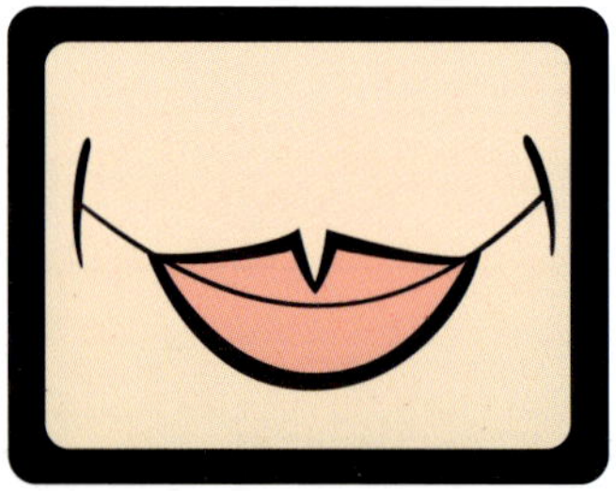

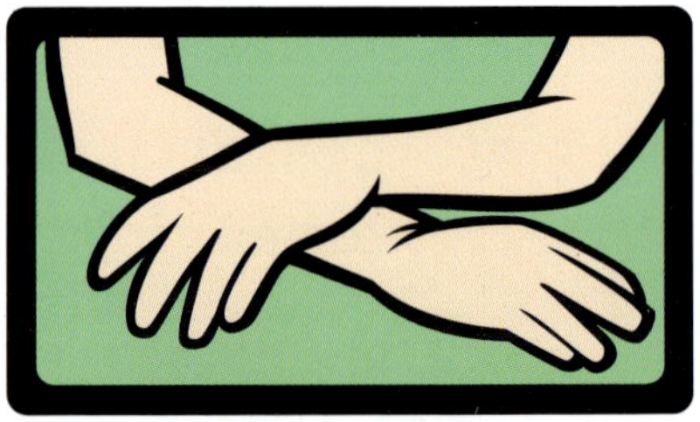

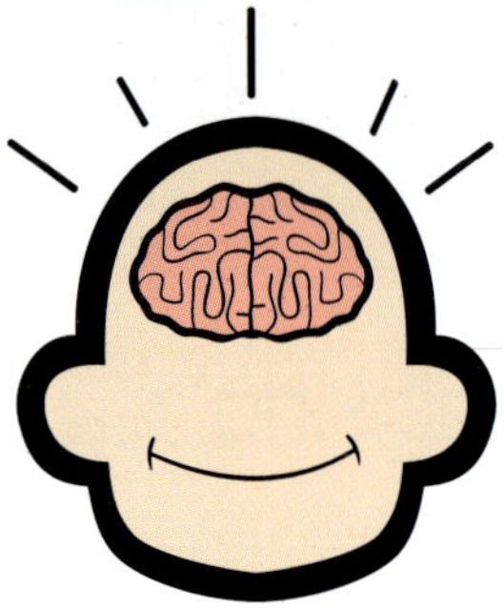